P9-DNG-722

NEW!

CELEBRITY Slouchy KNIT
BEANIES *for the family* Book 2

It's easy to resemble the rich and famous when you're wearing one of these slouchy beanies with casual-yet-confident style! They're quick to knit for everyone in the family with this fun collection of designs by Lisa Gentry.

LEISURE ARTS, INC. • Maumelle, Arkansas

BROKEN BARS

■■□□ **EASY**

SIZE INFORMATION

Small {Medium-Large}

Fits Head Circumference: 17{20-23}"/43{51-58.5} cm

Yarn (Bulky Weight)

[3.5 ounces, 120 yards
(100 grams, 110 meters) per skein]:

☐ 1 skein

Knitting Needles

16" (40.5 cm) Circular needles,

☐ Size 8 (5 mm) **and**

☐ Size 10½ (6.5 mm)
or sizes needed for gauge

Double pointed needles,

☐ Size 10½ (6.5 mm)

Additional Supplies

☐ Split-ring marker

☐ Yarn needle

Size Note: We have printed the instructions for the sizes in different colors to make it easier for you to find:

• Size Small in Blue
• Size Medium in Pink
• Size Large in Green

Instructions in Black apply to all sizes.

GAUGE INFORMATION

With larger size circular knitting needle, in Stockinette Stitch, 14 sts and 19 rows = 4" (10 cm)

TECHNIQUES USED

Knit Increase (*Figs. 7a & b, page 44*)

Purl Increase (*Fig. 8, page 45*)

K2 tog (*Fig. 9, page 45*)

Slip 1 as if to **knit**, K2 tog, PSSO (*Figs. 13a & b, page 46*)

P2 tog (*Fig. 14, page 47*)

P3 tog (*Fig. 15, page 47*)

INSTRUCTIONS
RIBBING

With smaller size circular knitting needle, cast on 68{72-76} sts; place a marker to mark the beginning of the round (*see Using Circular Knitting Needles and Markers, page 41*).

Rnd 1: (K1, P1) around.

Repeat Rnd 1 until Ribbing measures approximately 2" (5 cm) from cast on edge, increasing 30{26-22} sts evenly spaced on last rnd *(see Increasing Evenly, page 44)*: 98 sts.

BODY

Change to larger size circular knitting needle.

Rnds 1-3: (K1, P3, K1, P9) around.

Rnds 4-6: K1, P3, (K 11, P3) around to last 10 sts, K 10.

Rnds 7-9: (K1, P3, K1, P9) around.

Rnds 10-12: K8, P3, (K 11, P3) around to last 3 sts, K3.

Rnds 13-15: P7, K1, P3, K1, ★ P9, K1, P3, K1; repeat from ★ around to last 2 sts, P2.

Rnds 16-18: K8, P3, (K 11, P3) around to last 3 sts, K3.

SHAPING

Change to double pointed knitting needles when there are too few stitches to use a circular knitting needle 🎥 *(see Using Double Pointed Needles, page 42).*

Rnd 1: ★ K1, P3, K1, P2 tog, P7; repeat from ★ around: 91 sts.

Rnd 2: (K1, P3, K1, P8) around.

Rnd 3: ★ K1, P3, K1, P2 tog, P6; repeat from ★ around: 84 sts.

Rnd 4: K1, P3, (K9, P3) around to last 8 sts, K8.

Rnd 5: ★ K1, P3, K1, K2 tog, K3, K2 tog; repeat from ★ around: 70 sts.

Rnd 6: K1, P3, (K7, P3) around to last 6 sts, K6.

Rnd 7: (K1, P3, K1, P5) around.

Rnd 8: ★ K1, P2 tog, P1, K1, P5; repeat from ★ around: 63 sts.

Rnd 9: (K1, P2, K1, P5) around.

Rnd 10: K5, P3 tog, (K6, P3 tog) around to last st, K1: 49 sts.

Rnds 11 and 12: K5, P1, (K6, P1) around to last st, K1.

Rnd 13: ★ P2, P2 tog, K1, P1, K1; repeat from ★ around: 42 sts.

Rnds 14 and 15: (P3, K1, P1, K1) around.

Rnd 16: ★ P3, slip 1 as if to **knit**, K2 tog, PSSO; repeat from ★ around: 28 sts.

Rnd 17: (P3, K1) around.

Rnd 18: (P3 tog, K1) around: 14 sts.

Cut yarn leaving an 8" (20.5 cm) length for sewing. 📹 Thread yarn needle with end and slip remaining sts on Rnd 18 onto yarn needle; pull tightly to close and secure end.

CHECKERED

 **EASY**

SIZE INFORMATION

Small {Medium-Large}

Fits Head Circumference: 17{20-23}"/43{51-58.5} cm

SHOPPING LIST

Yarn (Super Bulky Weight) 🔳 **6** 🔳 SUPER BULKY

[6 ounces, 106 yards
(170 grams, 97 meters) per skein]:

- ☐ Pink - 1 skein
- ☐ Black - 1 skein

Knitting Needles

16" (40.5 cm) Circular needles,

- ☐ Size 11 (8 mm) **and**
- ☐ Size 9 (5.5 mm)

   or sizes needed for gauge

Double pointed needles,

- ☐ Size 11 (8 mm)

Additional Supplies

- ☐ Split-ring marker
- ☐ Yarn needle

Size Note: We have printed the instructions for the sizes in different colors to make it easier for you to find:

- Size Small in Blue
- Size Medium in Pink
- Size Large in Green

Instructions in Black apply to all sizes.

GAUGE INFORMATION

With larger size circular knitting
   needle, in pattern,
   8 sts and 14 rows = 3½" (9 cm)

TECHNIQUES USED

🎥 Knit Increase *(Figs. 7a & b, page 44)*
🎥 Purl Increase *(Fig. 8, page 45)*
🎥 K2 tog *(Fig. 9, page 45)*

INSTRUCTIONS
RIBBING

With smaller size circular knitting needle and Black, cast on 48{52-56} sts; place a marker to mark the beginning of the round 🎥 *(see Using Circular Knitting Needles and Markers, page 41).*

Rnd 1: (K1, P1) around.

Repeat Rnd 1 until Ribbing measures approximately 2¾" (7 cm) from cast on edge, increasing 0{4-0} sts evenly spaced on last rnd *(see Zeros, page 41 and Increasing Evenly, page 44)*; cut Black: 48{56-56} sts.

BODY

Change to larger size circular knitting needle.

Rnds 1 and 2: With Pink, (P2, K2) around.

Rnds 3 and 4: (K2, P2) around.

Rnds 5 thru 20{24-24}: Repeat Rnds 1-4, 4{5-5} times.

SHAPING

Change to double pointed knitting needles when there are too few stitches to use a circular knitting needle 🎥 *(see Using Double Pointed Needles, page 42).*

Rnd 1: (P2, K2, P2, K2 tog) around: 42{49-49} sts.

Rnd 2: (P2, K2, P2, K1) around.

Rnd 3: (K2, P2, K1, K2 tog) around: 36{42-42} sts.

Rnd 4: K2, P2, (K4, P2) around to last 2 sts, K2.

Rnd 5: (P2, K2, K2 tog) around: 30{35-35} sts.

Rnd 6: (P2, K3) around.

Rnd 7: (K2, P1, K2 tog) around: 24{28-28} sts.

Rnd 8: K2, P1, (K3, P1) around to last st, K1.

Rnd 9: (P2, K2 tog) around: 18{21-21} sts.

Rnd 10: (P2, K1) around.

Rnd 11: (K1, K2 tog) around: 12{14-14} sts.

Cut yarn leaving an 8" (20.5 cm) length for sewing. 🎥 Thread yarn needle with end and slip remaining sts on Rnd 11 onto yarn needle; pull **tightly** to close and secure end.

CHILD'S ROLLED BRIM

■■□□ **EASY**

SIZE INFORMATION

Small {Medium-Large}

Fits Head Circumference: 14{16-18}"/35.5{40.5-45.5} cm

Yarn (Bulky Weight) 🔵5

[5 ounces, 153 yards
(140 grams, 140 meters) per skein]:

☐ 1 skein

Knitting Needles

16" (40.5 cm) Circular needle,

☐ Size 11 (8 mm)

or size needed for gauge

Double pointed needles,

☐ Size 11 (8 mm)

Additional Supplies

☐ Split-ring marker

☐ Yarn needle

Size Note: We have printed the instructions for the sizes in different colors to make it easier for you to find:

• Size Small in Blue

• Size Medium in Pink

• Size Large in Green

Instructions in Black apply to all sizes.

GAUGE INFORMATION

In Stockinette Stitch,

12 sts and 16 rows = 4" (10 cm)

TECHNIQUE USED

🎥 K2 tog *(Fig. 9, page 45)*

INSTRUCTIONS
BODY

With circular knitting needle, cast on 42{48-54} sts; place a marker to mark the beginning of the round 🎥 *(see Using Circular Knitting Needles and Markers, page 41).*

Knit every rnd until Body measures approximately 7{7½-8}"/ 18{19-20.5} cm from cast on edge.

SHAPING

Change to double pointed knitting needles when there are too few stitches to use a circular needle 📹 *(see Using Double Pointed Needles, page 42).*

Rnd 1: ★ K5{6-7}, K2 tog; repeat from ★ around: 36{42-48} sts.

Rnd 2: Knit around.

Rnd 3: ★ K4{5-4}, K2 tog; repeat from ★ around: 30{36-40} sts.

Rnd 4: Knit around.

Rnd 5: ★ K3{4-3}, K2 tog; repeat from ★ around: 24{30-32} sts.

Rnd 6: Knit around.

Rnd 7: ★ K2{3-2}, K2 tog; repeat from ★ around: 18{24-24} sts.

Rnd 8: Knit around.

Rnd 9: ★ K1{2-2}, K2 tog; repeat from ★ around: 12{18-18} sts.

Cut yarn leaving an 8" (20.5 cm) length for sewing. 📹 Thread yarn needle with end and slip remaining sts on Rnd 9 onto needle; pull **tightly** to close and secure end.

Allow the bottom edge to roll.

CHILD'S GARTER RIDGES

 **EASY**

SIZE INFORMATION

Small {Medium-Large}

Fits Head Circumference: 14{16-18}"/35.5{40.5-45.5} cm

SHOPPING LIST

Yarn (Super Bulky Weight) 🔢 6

[3.5 ounces, 86 yards
(100 grams, 78 meters) per skein]:

☐ 1 skein

Knitting Needles

16" (40.5 cm) Circular needle,

☐ Size 11 (8 mm)

or size needed for gauge

Double pointed needles,

☐ Size 11 (8 mm)

Additional Supplies

☐ Split-ring marker

☐ Yarn needle

Size Note: We have printed the instructions for the sizes in different colors to make it easier for you to find:

• Size Small in Blue
• Size Medium in Pink
• Size Large in Green

Instructions in Black apply to all sizes.

GAUGE INFORMATION

In Garter Stitch,

  7 sts and 18 rows = 4" (10 cm)

TECHNIQUE USED

🎥 K2 tog *(Fig. 9, page 45)*

INSTRUCTIONS
BODY

With circular knitting needle, cast on 30{33-36} sts; place a marker to mark the beginning of the round 📹 *(see Using Circular Knitting Needles and Markers, page 41).*

Rnd 1: Knit around.

Rnd 2: Purl around.

Repeat Rnds 1 and 2 until Body measures approximately 7{7½-7½}"/ 18{19-19} cm from cast on edge.

SHAPING

Change to double pointed knitting needles when there are too few stitches to use a circular knitting needle 📹 *(see Using Double Pointed Needles, page 42).*

Rnd 1: ★ K4{9-4}, K2 tog; repeat from ★ around: 25{30-30} sts.

Rnd 2: Purl around.

Rnd 3: (K3, K2 tog) around: 20{24-24} sts.

Rnd 4: Purl around.

Rnd 5: (K2, K2 tog) around: 15{18-18} sts.

Rnd 6: Purl around.

Rnd 7: (K1, K2 tog) around: 10{12-12} sts.

Cut yarn leaving an 8" (20.5 cm) length for sewing. 📹 Thread yarn needle with end and slip remaining sts on Rnd 7 onto yarn needle; pull **tightly** to close and secure end.

Fold edge of Hat up 1½" (4 cm).

 EASY

SIZE INFORMATION

Small {Medium-Large}

Fits Head Circumference: 20{22-24}"/51{56-61} cm

SHOPPING LIST

Yarn (Super Bulky Weight) 🔵**6**
[6 ounces, 106 yards
(170 grams, 97 meters) per skein]:
☐ 1{1-2} skein(s)

Knitting Needles
16" (40.5 cm) Circular needle,
☐ Size 11 (8 mm)
  or size needed for gauge
Double pointed needles,
☐ Size 11 (8 mm)

Additional Supplies
☐ Split-ring marker
☐ Yarn needle

Size Note: We have printed the instructions for the sizes in different colors to make it easier for you to find:
• Size Small in Blue
• Size Medium in Pink
• Size Large in Green
Instructions in Black apply to all sizes.

GAUGE INFORMATION
In Stockinette Stitch,
  9 sts and 14 rows = 4" (10 cm)

TECHNIQUE USED
🎥 K2 tog *(Fig. 9, page 45)*

INSTRUCTIONS
BODY
With circular knitting needle, cast on 45{50-54} sts; place a marker to mark the beginning of the round 🎥 *(see Using Circular Knitting Needles and Markers, page 41).*

Knit every rnd until Body measures approximately 9½{9¾-10}"/ 24{25-25.5} cm from cast on edge.

SHAPING
Change to double pointed knitting needles when there are too few stitches to use a circular knitting needle 🎥 *(see Using Double Pointed Needles, page 42).*

Rnd 1: ★ K7{8-7}, K2 tog; repeat from ★ around: 40{45-48} sts.

Rnd 2: Knit around.

Rnd 3: ★ K6{7-6}, K2 tog; repeat from ★ around: 35{40-42} sts.

Rnd 4: Knit around.

Rnd 5: ★ K5{6-5}, K2 tog; repeat from ★ around: 30{35-36} sts.

Rnd 6: Knit around.

Rnd 7: ★ K4{5-4}, K2 tog; repeat from ★ around: 25{30-30} sts.

Rnd 8: Knit around.

Rnd 9: (K3, K2 tog) around: 20{24-24} sts.

Rnd 10: Knit around.

Rnd 11: K2 tog around: 10{12-12} sts.

Cut yarn leaving an 8" (20.5 cm) length for sewing. 📹 Thread yarn needle with end and slip remaining sts on Rnd 11 onto yarn needle; pull **tightly** to close and secure end.

Allow the bottom edge to roll.

RIBBED

 **EASY**

SIZE INFORMATION

Small {Medium-Large}

Fits Head Circumference: 17{20-23}"/43{51-58.5} cm

SHOPPING LIST

Yarn (Medium Weight) 🧶 **4**
[3.5 ounces, 170 yards
(100 grams, 156 meters) per skein]:
☐ 2 skeins

Knitting Needles
16" (40.5 cm) Circular needles,
☐ Size 7 (4.5 mm) **and**
☐ Size 9 (5.5 mm)
or sizes needed for gauge
Double pointed needles,
☐ Size 9 (5.5 mm)

Additional Supplies
☐ Split-ring marker
☐ Yarn needle

Size Note: We have printed the instructions for the sizes in different colors to make it easier for you to find:
- Size Small in Blue
- Size Medium in Pink
- Size Large in Green

Instructions in Black apply to all sizes.

GAUGE INFORMATION

With larger size circular knitting needle, in pattern,
16 sts and 32 rows = 4" (10 cm)

TECHNIQUES USED
🎥 K1 tbl *(Fig. 4, page 43)*
🎥 Slip 1 as if to **purl** *(Fig. 5, page 43)*
🎥 YO *(Figs. 6a & b, pages 42 & 43)*
🎥 K2 tog *(Fig. 9, page 45)*
🎥 K4 tog *(Fig. 11, page 45)*
🎥 P2 tog *(Fig. 14, page 47)*

INSTRUCTIONS
BAND

With smaller size circular knitting needle, cast on 13 sts.

Row 1: K1 tbl, P1, (K1, P1) 5 times, with yarn in **front**, slip 1 as if to **purl**.

Row 2: K1 tbl, K1, (P1, K1) 5 times, with yarn in **front**, slip 1 as if to **purl**.

Repeat Rows 1 and 2 until Band measures approximately 16{19-22}"/ 40.5{48.5-56} cm from cast on edge.

Bind off all sts in pattern, leaving a long end for sewing.

Thread yarn needle with long end and sew cast on edge and bound off edge together.

BODY

With larger size circular knitting needle and beginning at seam, pick up 90 sts around working in ends of rows on Band 📹 *(Fig. 16, page 47)*; place a marker to mark beginning of the round 📹 *(see Circular Knitting Needles and Markers, page 41)*.

When instructed to slip a stitch, with yarn at **back**, slip it as if to **purl**.

Rnd 1: (K1, YO, slip 1) around: 135 sts.

Rnd 2: ★ YO, slip 1, P2 tog (YO and slipped st); repeat from ★ around.

Rnd 3: ★ K2 tog (YO and slipped st), YO, slip 1; repeat from ★ around.

Repeat Rnds 2 and 3 until piece measures approximately 6½{6¾-7}"/ 16.5{17-18} cm from bottom edge of Band, ending by working Rnd 3.

SHAPING

Change to double pointed knitting needles when there are too few stitches to use a circular needle 📹 *(see Using Double Pointed Needles, page 42)*.

Rnd 1: ★ YO, K4 tog, P2 tog, (YO, slip 1, P2 tog) 7 times; repeat from ★ around: 120 sts.

Rnd 2: ★ K2 tog, YO, slip 1; repeat from ★ around.

Rnd 3: ★ YO, slip 1, P2 tog; repeat from ★ around.

Rnds 4-6: Repeat Rnds 2 and 3 once, then repeat Rnd 2 once **more**.

Rnd 7: ★ YO, K4 tog, P2 tog, (YO, slip 1, P2 tog) 6 times; repeat from ★ around: 105 sts.

Rnd 8: ★ K2 tog, YO, slip 1; repeat from ★ around.

Rnd 9: ★ YO, slip 1, P2 tog; repeat from ★ around.

Rnd 10: ★ K2 tog, YO, slip 1; repeat from ★ around.

Rnd 11: ★ YO, K4 tog, P2 tog, (YO, slip 1, P2 tog) 5 times; repeat from ★ around: 90 sts.

Rnd 12: ★ K2 tog, YO, slip 1; repeat from ★ around.

Rnd 13: ★ YO, slip 1, P2 tog; repeat from ★ around.

Rnd 14: ★ K2 tog, YO, slip 1; repeat from ★ around.

Rnd 15: ★ YO, K4 tog, P2 tog, (YO, slip 1, P2 tog) 4 times; repeat from ★ around: 75 sts.

Rnd 16: ★ K2 tog, YO, slip 1; repeat from ★ around.

Rnd 17: ★ YO, slip 1, P2 tog; repeat from ★ around.

Rnd 18: ★ K2 tog, YO, slip 1; repeat from ★ around.

Rnd 19: ★ YO, K4 tog, P2 tog, (YO, slip 1, P2 tog) 3 times; repeat from ★ around: 60 sts.

Rnd 20: (K2 tog, P1) around: 40 sts.

Rnd 21: (K1, P1) around.

Cut yarn leaving an 8" (20.5 cm) length for sewing. 🎥 Thread yarn needle with end and slip remaining sts on Rnd 21 onto yarn needle; pull **tightly** to close and secure end.

SIMPLE RIB

EASY

SIZE INFORMATION

Small {Medium-Large}

Fits Head Circumference: 17{20-23}"/43{51-58.5} cm

SHOPPING LIST

Yarn (Super Bulky Weight) 🔵 6

[3.5 ounces, 108 yards
(100 grams, 99 meters) per skein]:

☐ 1 skein

Knitting Needles

16" (40.5 cm) Circular needles,

☐ Size 11 (8 mm) **and**

☐ Size 9 (5.5 mm)

or sizes needed for gauge

Double pointed needles,

☐ Size 11 (8 mm)

Additional Supplies

☐ Split-ring marker

☐ Yarn needle

Size Note: We have printed the instructions for the sizes in different colors to make it easier for you to find:

• Size Small in Blue

• Size Medium in Pink

• Size Large in Green

Instructions in Black apply to all sizes.

GAUGE INFORMATION

With larger size circular knitting needle, in Stockinette Stitch, 11 sts and 14 rows = 4" (10 cm)

TECHNIQUES USED

🎥 Knit Increase *(Figs. 7a & b, page 44)*

🎥 Purl Increase *(Fig. 8, page 45)*

🎥 K2 tog *(Fig. 9, page 45)*

INSTRUCTIONS
RIBBING

With smaller size circular knitting needle, cast on 60{64-68} sts; place a marker to mark the beginning of the round 🎥 *(see Using Circular Knitting Needles and Markers, page 41)*.

Rnd 1: (K2, P2) around.

Repeat Rnd 1 until Ribbing measures approximately 4½" (11.5 cm) from cast on edge, increasing 6{8-4} sts evenly spaced on last rnd *(see Increasing Evenly, page 44)*: 66{72-72} sts.

BODY

Change to larger size circular knitting needle.

Knit every rnd until piece measures approximately 8½{8¾-9}"/ 21.5{22-23} cm from cast on edge.

SHAPING

Change to double pointed knitting needles when there are too few stitches to use a circular knitting needle 📹 *(see Using Double Pointed Needles, page 42)*.

Rnd 1: (K4, K2 tog) around: 55{60-60} sts.

Rnd 2: Knit around.

Rnd 3: (K3, K2 tog) around: 44{48-48} sts.

Rnd 4: Knit around.

Rnd 5: (K2, K2 tog) around: 33{36-36} sts.

Rnd 6: Knit around.

Rnd 7: (K1, K2 tog) around: 22{24-24} sts.

Rnd 8: Knit around.

Rnd 9: K2 tog around: 11{12-12} sts.

Cut yarn leaving an 8" (20.5 cm) length for sewing. 📹 Thread yarn needle with end and slip remaining sts on Rnd 9 onto yarn needle; pull **tightly** to close and secure end.

 **EASY**

SIZE INFORMATION

Small {Medium-Large}

Fits Head Circumference: 17{19½-22}"/43{49.5-56} cm

Size Note: We have printed the instructions for the sizes in different colors to make it easier for you to find:

• Size Small in Blue
• Size Medium in Pink
• Size Large in Green

Instructions in Black apply to all sizes.

GAUGE INFORMATION

With larger size circular knitting needle, in Stockinette Stitch, 17 sts and 24 rows = 4" (10 cm)

TECHNIQUES USED

🎥 K2 tog *(Fig. 9, page 45)*
🎥 P2 tog *(Fig. 14, page 47)*

INSTRUCTIONS
BRIM

With smaller size circular knitting needle and Purple, cast on 80{92-104} sts; place a marker to mark the beginning of the round 🎥 *(see Using Circular Knitting Needles and Markers, page 41).*

Rnd 1: Purl around.

Rnd 2: Knit around.

Rnds 3-5: Repeat Rnds 1 and 2 once, then repeat Rnd 1 once **more**.

Cut Purple.

BODY

Change to larger size circular knitting needle.

Rnds 1-10: With Variegated, knit around.

Cut Variegated.

Rnd 11: With Purple, knit around.

Rnds 12-15: Purl around.

Cut Purple.

Rnds 16-60: Repeat Rnds 1-15, 3 times.

Cut Purple.

SHAPING

Change to double pointed knitting needles when there are too few stitches to use a circular knitting needle 🎥 *(see Using Double Pointed Needles, page 42).*

Rnd 1: With Variegated, K 26{21-22}, K2 tog, ★ K 24{21-18}, K2 tog; repeat from ★ 1{2-3} time(s) **more:** 77{88-99} sts.

Rnds 2 and 3: Knit around.

Rnd 4: ★ K5{6-7}, K2 tog; repeat from ★ around: 66{77-88} sts.

Rnds 5 and 6: Knit around.

Rnd 7: ★ K4{5-6}, K2 tog; repeat from ★ around: 55{66-77} sts.

Rnd 8: Knit around.

Rnd 9: ★ K3{4-5}, K2 tog; repeat from ★ around: 44{55-66} sts.

Rnd 10: Knit around.

Cut Variegated.

Rnd 11: With Purple, knit around.

Rnd 12: Purl around.

Rnd 13: ★ P2{3-4}, P2 tog; repeat from ★ around: 33{44-55} sts.

Rnds 14 and 15: Purl around.

Cut Purple.

Rnd 16: With Variegated, ★ K1{2-3}, K2 tog; repeat from ★ around: 22{33-44} sts.

Rnds 17 and 18: Knit around.

Rnd 19: K 0{1-0} *(see Zeros, page 41)*, K2 tog around: 11{17-22} sts.

Cut yarn leaving an 8" (20.5 cm) length for sewing.  Thread yarn needle with end and slip remaining sts on Rnd 19 onto yarn needle; pull **tightly** to close and secure end.

TEXTURED STRIPES

 **EASY**

SIZE INFORMATION

Small {Medium-Large}

Fits Head Circumference: 17{20-23}"/43{51-58.5} cm

SHOPPING LIST

Yarn (Medium Weight)

[3.5 ounces, 210 yards
(100 grams, 192 meters) per skein]:

☐ Grey - 1 skein

☐ Blue - 1 skein

Knitting Needles

16" (40.5 cm) Circular needles,

☐ Size 7 (4.5 mm) **and**

☐ Size 8 (5 mm)

or sizes needed for gauge

Double pointed needles,

☐ Size 8 (5 mm)

Additional Supplies

☐ Split-ring marker

☐ Yarn needle

Size Note: We have printed the instructions for the sizes in different colors to make it easier for you to find:

• Size Small in Blue

• Size Medium in Pink

• Size Large in Green

Instructions in Black apply to all sizes.

GAUGE INFORMATION

With larger size circular knitting needle, in Stockinette Stitch,
18 sts and 22 rows = 4" (10 cm)

TECHNIQUES USED

🎥 YO *(Fig. 6a, page 44)*

🎥 Knit Increase *(Figs. 7a & b, page 44)*

🎥 Purl Increase *(Fig. 8, page 45)*

🎥 K2 tog tbl *(Fig. 10, page 45)*

🎥 Slip 1 as if to knit, K1, PSSO
(Figs. 12a & b, page 46)

INSTRUCTIONS
RIBBING

With smaller size circular knitting needle and Grey, cast on 84{90-96} sts; place a marker to mark the beginning of the round 🎥 *(see Using Circular Knitting Needles and Markers, page 41)*.

Rnd 1: (K1, P1) around.

Repeat Rnd 1 until Ribbing measures approximately 2" (5 cm) from cast on edge, increasing 24{26-20} sts evenly spaced on last rnd *(see Increasing Evenly, page 41)*: 108{116-116} sts.

Cut Grey.

BODY

Change to larger size circular knitting needle.

Rnds 1-5: With Blue, knit around.

Cut Blue.

Rnd 6: With Grey, (K2 tog tbl, YO) around.

Rnd 7: Knit around.

Rnds 8-10: Repeat Rnds 6 and 7 once, then repeat Rnd 6 once **more**.

Cut Grey.

Rnds 11-15: With Blue, knit around.

Cut Blue.

Rnd 16: With Grey, knit around.

Rnd 17: (K2 tog tbl, YO) around.

Rnd 18: Knit around.

Rnd 19: (K2 tog tbl, YO) around.

Rnd 20: Knit around; cut Grey.

Rnds 21-28: With Blue, knit around.

Cut Blue.

Rnds 28 and 29: With Grey, knit around.

Rnd 30: (K2 tog tbl, YO) around.

Rnds 31 and 32: Knit around.

Cut Grey.

Rnd 33: With Blue, knit around.

SHAPING

Change to double pointed knitting needles when there are too few stitches to use a circular knitting needle 🎥 *(see Using Double Pointed Needles, page 42)*.

Rnd 1: K 15{9-9}, slip 1 as if to **knit**, K1, PSSO, ★ K 11{5-5}, slip 1 as if to **knit**, K1, PSSO; repeat from ★ around: 100 sts.

Rnds 2 and 3: Knit around.

Rnd 4: ★ K8, slip 1 as if to **knit**, K1, PSSO; repeat from ★ around: 90 sts.

Rnds 5 and 6: Knit around.

Rnd 7: ★ K7, slip 1 as if to **knit**, K1, PSSO; repeat from ★ around: 80 sts.

Rnds 8 and 9: Knit around.

Cut Blue.

Rnd 10: With Grey, knit around.

Rnd 11: ★ K6, slip 1 as if to **knit**, K1, PSSO; repeat from ★ around: 70 sts.

Rnds 12 and 13: Knit around.

Rnd 14: ★ K5, slip 1 as if to **knit**, K1, PSSO; repeat from ★ around: 60 sts.

Rnds 15 and 16: Knit around.

Cut Grey.

Rnd 17: With Blue, ★ K4, slip 1 as if to **knit**, K1, PSSO; repeat from ★ around: 50 sts.

Rnd 18: Knit around.

Rnd 19: ★ K3, slip 1 as if to **knit**, K1, PSSO; repeat from ★ around: 40 sts.

Rnd 20: Knit around.

Rnd 21: ★ K2, slip 1 as if to **knit**, K1, PSSO; repeat from ★ around: 30 sts.

Rnd 22: Knit around.

Rnd 23: ★ K1, slip 1 as if to **knit**, K1, PSSO; repeat from ★ around: 20 sts.

Rnd 24: Knit around.

Cut yarn leaving an 8" (20.5 cm) length for sewing. Thread yarn needle with end and slip remaining sts on Rnd 24 onto yarn needle; pull **tightly** to close and secure end.

GENERAL INSTRUCTIONS

ABBREVIATIONS

cm	centimeters
K	knit
mm	millimeters
P	purl
PSSO	pass slipped st over
Rnd(s)	Round(s)
st(s)	stitch(es)
tbl	through back loop
tog	together
YO	yarn over

SYMBOLS & TERMS

★ — work instructions following ★ as many **more** times as indicated in addition to the first time.

( ) or **[ ]** — work enclosed instructions **as many** times as specified by the number immediately following **or** work all enclosed instructions in the stitch or space indicated **or** contains explanatory remarks.

colon (:) — the number(s) given after a colon at the end of a row or round denote(s) the number of stitches you should have on that row or round.

KNIT TERMINOLOGY

UNITED STATES		INTERNATIONAL
gauge	=	tension
bind off	=	cast off
yarn over (YO)	=	yarn forward (yfwd) **or**
		yarn around needle (yrn)

Yarn Weight Symbol & Names	LACE 0	SUPER FINE 1	FINE 2	LIGHT 3	MEDIUM 4	BULKY 5	SUPER BULKY 6
Type of Yarns in Category	Fingering, size 10 crochet thread	Sock, Fingering, Baby	Sport, Baby	DK, Light Worsted	Worsted, Afghan, Aran	Chunky, Craft, Rug	Bulky, Roving
Knit Gauge Range* in Stockinette St to 4" (10 cm)	33-40** sts	27-32 sts	23-26 sts	21-24 sts	16-20 sts	12-15 sts	6-11 sts
Advised Needle Size Range	000-1	1 to 3	3 to 5	5 to 7	7 to 9	9 to 11	11 and larger

*GUIDELINES ONLY: The chart above reflects the most commonly used gauges and needle sizes for specific yarn categories.

** Lace weight yarns are usually knitted on larger needles to create lacy openwork patterns. Accordingly, a gauge range is difficult to determine. Always follow the gauge stated in your pattern.

■□□□ BEGINNER	Projects for first-time knitters using basic knit and purl stitches. Minimal shaping.
■■□□ EASY	Projects using basic stitches, repetitive stitch patterns, simple color changes, and simple shaping and finishing.
■■■□ INTERMEDIATE	Projects with a variety of stitches, such as basic cables and lace, simple intarsia, double-pointed needles and knitting in the round needle techniques, mid-level shaping and finishing.
■■■■ EXPERIENCED	Projects using advanced techniques and stitches, such as short rows, fair isle, more intricate intarsia, cables, lace patterns, and numerous color changes.

KNITTING NEEDLES

U.S.	0	1	2	3	4	5	6	7	8	9	10	10½	11	13	15	17	19	35	50
U.K.	13	12	11	10	9	8	7	6	5	4	3	2	1	00	000	---	---	---	---
Metric - mm	2	2.25	2.75	3.25	3.5	3.75	4	4.5	5	5.5	6	6.5	8	9	10	12.75	15	19	25

GAUGE

Exact gauge is **essential** for proper size. Before beginning your project, make a sample swatch in the yarn and needle specified in the individual instructions. After completing the swatch, measure it, counting your stitches and rows carefully. If your swatch is larger or smaller than specified, **make another, changing needle size to get the correct gauge**. Keep trying until you find the size needles that will give you the specified gauge.

SIZING

To determine what size to make, measure around the crown of your head with a tape measure *(Fig. 1)*. As long as the Beanie is made from a yarn with elasticity, the fabric will have some give. You want the band to fit snugly, so choose the size closest to your measurement or slightly smaller. You can also adjust the band size by changing the needle size used for it, and therefore adjusting the gauge and the finished measurement.

Fig. 1

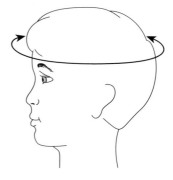

MARKERS

As a convenience to you, we have used markers to help distinguish the beginning of a round. Place a marker around the first stitch. You may use a purchased split-ring marker or place a length of contrasting color yarn around the stitch. Move it up at the end of each round; remove it when no longer needed.

ZEROS

To consolidate the lengh of an involved pattern, zeros are sometimes used so that all sizes can be combined. For example, K 0{1-0} means that the first and third sizes would do nothing, and the second size would K1.

KNITTING IN THE ROUND
USING CIRCULAR KNITTING NEEDLES

When you knit a tube as for a hat, you are going to work around on the outside of a circle, with the right side of the knitting facing you. Using a circular knitting needle, cast on all stitches as instructed. Untwist and straighten the stitches on the needle to be sure that the cast on ridge lies on the inside of the needle and never rolls around the needle.

Hold the needle so that the ball of yarn is attached to the stitch closest to the **right** hand point. Place a marker to mark the beginning of the round.

To begin working in the round, knit the stitches on the left hand point *(Fig. 2)*.

Fig. 2

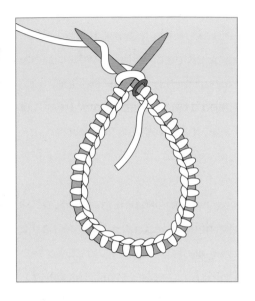

Continue working each round as instructed **without turning the work**; but for the first three rounds or so, check to be sure that the cast on edge has not twisted around the needle. If it has, it is impossible to untwist it. The only way to fix this is to rip it out and return to the cast on row.

USING DOUBLE POINTED KNITTING NEEDLES

When working a piece that is too small to use a circular knitting needle, double pointed knitting needles are required. Divide the stitches into thirds and slip one-third of the stitches onto each of 3 double pointed needles, forming a triangle. With the fourth needle, knit across the stitches on the first needle *(Fig. 3)*. You will now have an empty needle with which to knit the stitches from the next needle. Work the first stitch of each needle firmly to prevent gaps. Continue working around without turning the work.

Fig. 3

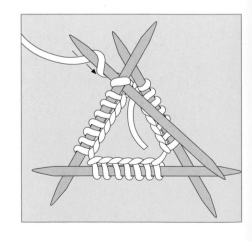

KNIT 1 THROUGH BACK LOOP *(abbreviated K1 tbl)*

Knit into the back of the first stitch on the left needle *(Fig. 4)*.

Fig. 4

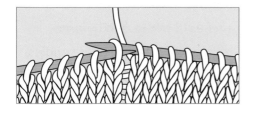

SLIP 1 AS IF TO PURL

When instructed to "slip 1 as if to **purl**," insert the right needle from **right** to **left** into the first stitch on the left needle *(Fig. 5)* and slip stitch onto the right needle.

Fig. 5

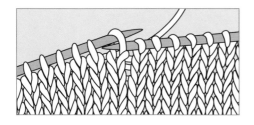

YARN OVER *(abbreviated YO)*

A yarn over is simply placing the working strand over the right needle creating an extra stitch. Since the yarn over produces a hole in the knit fabric, it is used for a lacy effect. On the row following a yarn over, you must be careful to keep it on the needle and treat it as a stitch by knitting or purling it as instructed.

To make a yarn over, you'll loop the working strand over the needle like you would to knit or purl a stitch, bringing it either to the front or to the back of the piece so that it'll be ready to work the next stitch, creating a new stitch on the needle.

After a knit stitch, before a knit stitch

Bring the yarn forward **between** the needles, then back **over** the top of the right hand needle, so that it is now in position to **knit** the next stitch *(Fig. 6a)*.

Fig. 6a

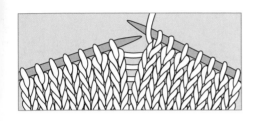

After a purl stitch, before a purl stitch

Take yarn **over** the right hand needle to the back, then forward **under** it, so that it is now in position to **purl** the next stitch *(Fig. 6b)*.

Fig. 6b

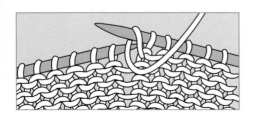

INCREASES
INCREASING EVENLY

Divide the number of increases required into the number of stitches on the needle. Subtract one from the result and the new number is the approximate number of stitches to be worked between each increase. Adjust the number as needed.

KNIT INCREASE

Knit the next stitch but do **not** slip the old stitch off the left needle *(Fig. 7a)*. Insert the right needle into the back loop of the same stitch and **knit** it *(Fig. 7b)*, then slip the old stitch off the left needle.

Fig. 7a   **Fig. 7b**

PURL INCREASE

Purl the next stitch but do **not** slip the old stitch off the left needle. Insert the right needle into the back loop of the same stitch from **back** to **front** *(Fig. 8)* and **purl** it. Slip the old stitch off the left needle.

Fig. 8

KNIT 2 TOGETHER THROUGH BACK LOOP

(abbreviated K2 tog tbl)

Insert the right needle into the **back** of the first two stitches on the left needle *(Fig. 10)*, then **knit** them together as if they were one stitch.

Fig. 10

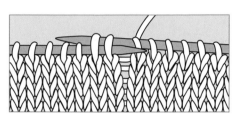

DECREASES
KNIT 2 TOGETHER

(abbreviated K2 tog)

Insert the right needle into the **front** of the first two stitches on the left needle as if to **knit** *(Fig. 9)*, then **knit** them together as if they were one stitch.

Fig. 9

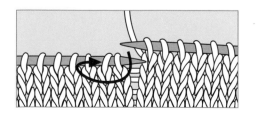

KNIT 4 TOGETHER

(abbreviated K4 tog)

Insert the right needle into the **front** of the first four stitches on the left needle as if to **knit** *(Fig. 11)*, then **knit** them together as if they were one stitch.

Fig. 11

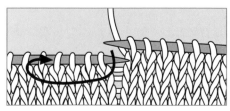

SLIP 1, KNIT 1, PASS SLIPPED STITCH OVER

(abbreviated slip 1, K1, PSSO)

Slip one stitch as if to **knit** *(Fig. 12a)*. Knit the next stitch. With the left needle, bring the slipped stitch over the knit stitch just made *(Fig. 12b)* and off the needle.

Fig. 12a

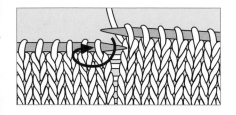

Fig. 12b

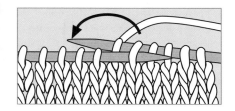

SLIP 1, KNIT 2 TOGETHER, PASS SLIPPED STITCH OVER

(abbreviated slip 1, K2 tog, PSSO)

Slip one stitch as if to **knit** *(Fig. 13a)*. Knit the next two stitches together *(Fig. 9, page 45)*. With the left needle, bring the slipped stitch over the stitch just made *(Fig. 13b)* and off the needle.

Fig. 13a

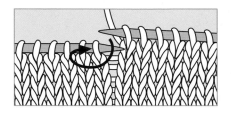

Fig. 13b

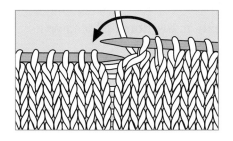

PURL 2 TOGETHER

(abbreviated P2 tog)

Insert the right needle into the **front** of the first two stitches on the left needle as if to **purl** *(Fig. 14)*, then **purl** them together as if they were one stitch.

Fig. 14

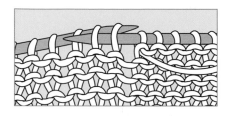

PURL 3 TOGETHER

(abbreviated P3 tog)

Insert the right needle into the **front** of the first three stitches on the left needle as if to **purl** *(Fig. 15)*, then **purl** them together as if they were one stitch.

Fig. 15

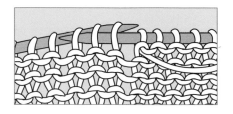

PICKING UP STITCHES

When instructed to pick up stitches, insert the needle from the **front** to the **back** under two strands at the edge of the worked piece *(Fig. 16)*. Put the yarn around the needle as if to **knit**, then bring the needle with the yarn back through the stitch to the right side, resulting in a stitch on the needle.

Repeat this along the edge, picking up the required number of stitches. A crochet hook may be helpful to pull yarn through.

Fig. 16

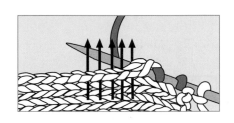

YARN INFORMATION

The Beanies in this book were made using various weights of yarn. Any brand of the specified weight of yarn may be used. It is best to refer to the yardage/meters when determining how many balls or skeins to purchase. Remember, to arrive at the finished size, it is the GAUGE/TENSION that is important, not the brand of yarn.

For your convenience, listed below are the specific yarns used to create our photography models.

BROKEN BARS
Bernat® Alpaca™
#93420 Peony

CHECKERED
Lion Brand®
   Wool-Ease®
   Thick & Quick®
Pink - #112 Raspberry
Black - #153 Black

CHILD'S ROLLED BRIM
Lion Brand®
   Wool-Ease® Chunky
#155 Silver Grey

CHILD'S GARTER RIDGES
Bernat® Baby Blanket™
#03005 White

MAN'S ROLLED BRIM
Lion Brand®
   Wool-Ease®
   Thick & Quick®
#124 Barley

RIBBED
Lion Brand® Vanna's Choice®
#125 Taupe

SIMPLE RIB
Bernat® Softee® Chunky
#28047 Grey Ragg

STRIPES
Patons® Classic Wool Worsted
Purple - #77307 Plum Heather
Variegated - #77414 Rosewood

TEXTURED STRIPES
Patons® Classic Wool Worsted
Grey - #77044 Mercury
Blue - #77132 Royal Blue